Teeny Tiny Pieces

MARIA DILLON

Copyright © 2022 Homestead Mentor Publishing
All rights reserved.
ISBN: 979-8-9860373-0-1

To My Sweet Lucie
Thank you for adding the pink to my blue,
the extra to our extraordinary, and helping
to bring sense to our nonsense.
You
Inspire
Me.

ACKNOWLEDGMENTS

If Ms. Conner had not invited me to join Lucie's kindergarten class to celebrate World Down Syndrome Day, this book would still have been sitting in my draft folder. I am so grateful for her and all of Lucie's teachers and aides that care so much for her. They have each played a significant role in cultivating Lucie's love of school!

When I reached out to the incredible Down Syndrome community asking for photos, I was inundated with hundreds of the most incredible photos of the cutest humans on the planet! I am grateful that they all took the time to share their pictures and their children with me so that I could, in turn, share them with you!

Thank you to my four boys, who helped inspire me to write this. I wanted Lucie's siblings and peers to understand that she was different, but not better than them, which is an important building block for strong friendships.

But mostly, I want to thank my husband. He always said I would write a book one day. Thank you for all of your love and (tech) support! I love you!

When a person is made, they are all made uniquely,
Out of teeny tiny pieces that are matched up quite neatly.

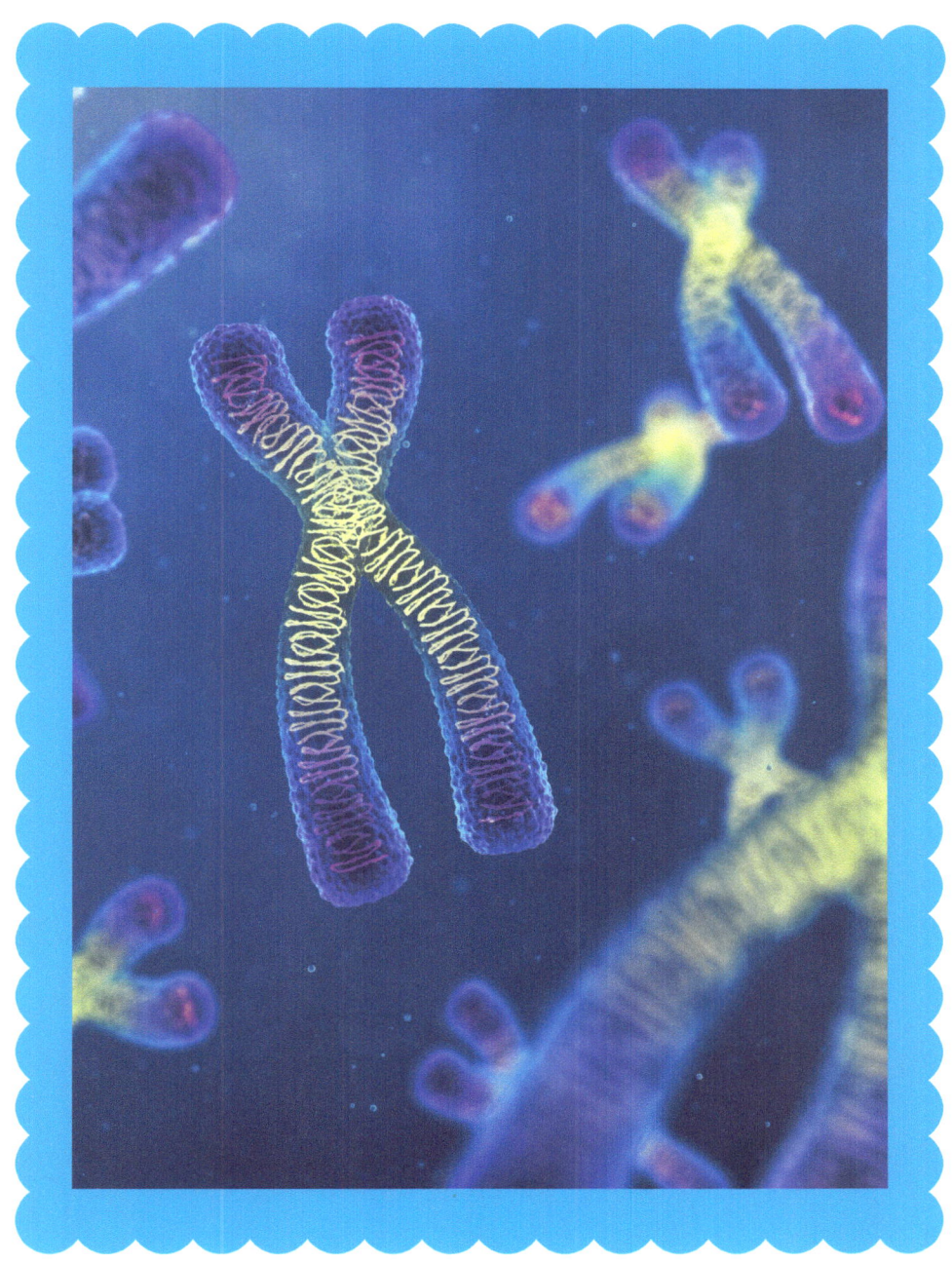

These teeny tiny pieces that you really can't see,

Are what makes you, you...

And what makes me, me!

These little pieces, called chromosomes, are found everywhere!

They determine things like the color of your hair.

We each have 23 pairs of them in every single cell.

And those tiny things control what stuff might be hard...

and what stuff we do well.

Are your eyes blue like the ocean?

Or are they dark brown?

Can you roll your tongue like this?

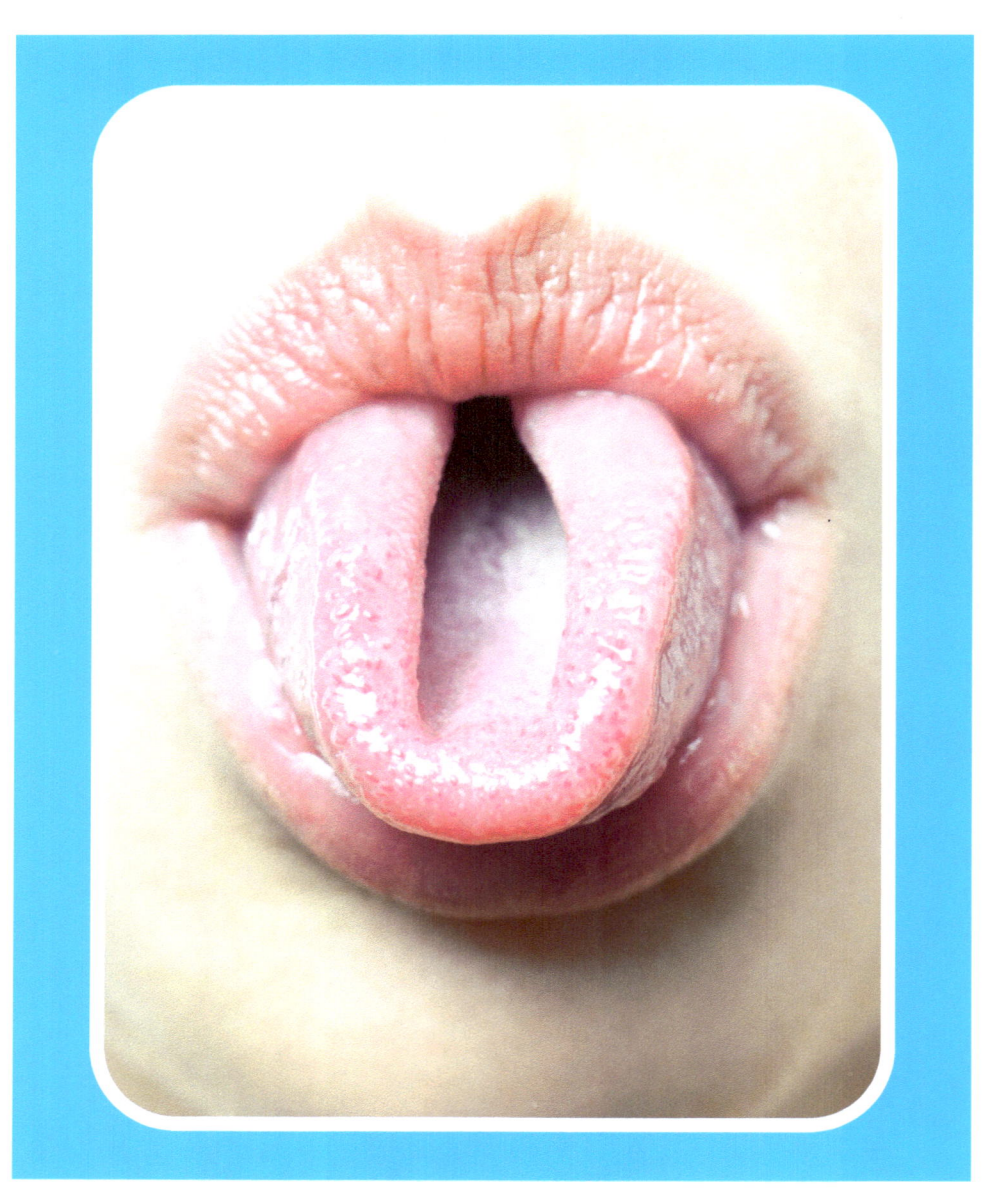

Does your nose point up or down?

Does your skin look darker in summer or does the sun turn you red?

Chromosomes tell us lots of things from our toes...

...to our heads.

Twenty-three pairs makes 46 in almost everyone.

But, every once in a while, a baby gets 46... plus one!

When that happens, it's okay. No need to freak out.

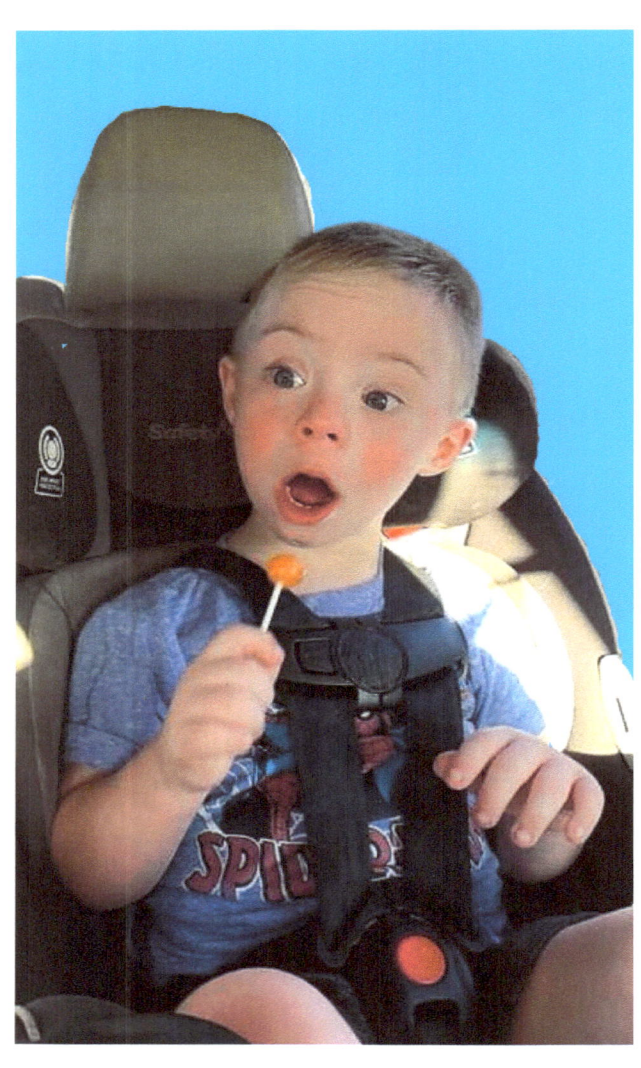

It's what we call Down Syndrome. It's exciting, no doubt!

People with a bonus piece are just like you and me.

They like markers,

swimming pools,

...and they love ice cream!

They have feelings,

like new friends,

and love to play games!

They like to dance,

run around,

and don't like being called names.

You say, "That isn't very different and seems just like me!"

So, let's talk about some things that might be easier to see.

Sometimes they have features that are easy to spot.

Like their eyes have an almond shape, more often than not.

Learning to walk can be harder when they are just small.

But with lots of hard work they can play tag with you all.

And while they might have oodles and oodles to say,

They might need to communicate in a different way.

They take a little longer to learn their A's, B's, and C's,

But friendships, hugs, and smiles- they get A's in all these!

They do have feelings and they can feel sad.

They are not perfect! They make mistakes and get mad.

What they want is the same as every girl and every boy.

They want good days full of happiness and lots of moments of joy.

They want to love. They want to learn. They need to know they're protected.

And when they're with friends, they want to feel accepted.

So, if you see someone that looks a little like her, don't leave them alone!

There's no need to be scared of an extra chromosome.

Ask if they need help or a friend, since this much is true...

They are made up of teeny tiny pieces, just like YOU!

ABOUT THE AUTHOR

After getting a degree in special education and teaching for a couple of years, Maria knew that something was missing. She ultimately found herself authoring behavior support plans for adults with developmental delays and this is where she uncovered her love of writing. She married in 2006 and children came soon after. She gladly chose to stay home with her growing family, but never quite gave up on her love of writing. She blogged her journey with infertility and miscarriages and then, when Lucie arrived, the focus of her writing turned to her unexpected journey of parenting a baby girl born with a bonus chromosome. As her family continued to grow, her time for writing shrunk. In the start of 2022, she began carving out time to write, once again. This is her first book and she hopes that there are more in the future.

She has 5 children and Lucie is her only girl!

I would love to hear from you!
47teenytinypieces.com

www.ingramcontent.com/pod-product-compliance
Lightning Source LLC
Chambersburg PA
CBHW061030180426
43192CB00034B/75